KNOWING THE
TRUTH ABOUT

The
Reliability
of the Bible

John Ankerberg
& John Weldon

HARVEST HOUSE PUBLISHERS
Eugene, Oregon 97402

Verses marked NASB are taken from the New American Standard Bible, © 1960, 1962, 1963, 1968, 1971, 1972, 1973, 1975, 1977 by The Lockman Foundation. Used by permission.

Verses marked NIV are taken from the Holy Bible, New International Version ®. Copyright © 1973, 1978, 1984 by the International Bible Society. Used by permission of Zondervan Publishing House. The "NIV" and "New International Version" trademarks are registered in the United States Patent and Trademark Office by International Bible Society.

Cover design by Terry Dugan Design, Minneapolis Minnesota.

Other booklets by
John Ankerberg and
John Weldon

**KNOWING THE TRUTH ABOUT
THE RELIABILITY OF THE BIBLE**

Copyright © 1997 by the John Ankerberg Show
Published by Harvest House Publishers
Eugene, Oregon 97402

ISBN 1-56507-793-8

Printed in the United States of America.

98 99 00 01 02 / LP / 10 9 8 7 6 5 4 3 2 1

Contents

The Crucial Subject

The Bible is clearly the most influential book the world has ever known. Abraham Lincoln called it "the best gift God has given to man." Patrick Henry said, "It is worth all other books which were ever printed." Noted British statesman William Gladstone wrote that "an immeasurable distance separates it from all competitors" while the famous philosopher Immanuel Kant declared, "The Bible is the greatest benefit which the human race has ever experienced." A. M. Sullivan observed, "The cynic who ignores, ridicules, or denies the Bible, spurning its spiritual rewards and aesthetic excitement, contributes to his own moral anemia."[1]

Why do we think the subject of this book, the reliability of the Bible, is such a crucial subject? Because of its implications. Throughout human history virtually all people have searched for God at some point in their lives, because apart from God they intuitively sensed that their lives lacked ultimate meaning. Yet the Bible claims to be the revealed Word of God to man (John 1:12,13; 3:16; 17:3; 1 John 5:9-15). Further, it tells us how we may come to know God personally. If the Bible is true, then in its pages we can find ultimate meaning for our lives and the God we have searched for. We can read of His mighty and gracious acts among people and nations in the Old Testament, and we can especially see His love and compassion in the New Testament. For it is undeniably true that if we want to know who God really is, and what He is really like, we need only look at Jesus Christ (John 14:6-11; 12:44,45).

Unfortunately, many people today do not believe in the one true God, and they deny that God has personally revealed Himself in the Bible. They have spawned skeptical theories and written endless volumes attacking the idea that the Bible is an accurate account of God's intervention in human history and that it reveals His will for man. But even skeptics cannot deny that the Bible's influence in history is incalculable and that it has literally changed our world—not just Western history, but all of history.

The topic of this book is vital because if there is solid evidence that the Bible is God's Word to us, its critics are wrong. Worse, they are leading astray all those who listen to them. If the Bible alone is divine revelation, then by definition it is the most important Book in the world. It alone will tell us what God requires of us.

In light of these undeniable facts, to be ignorant of the Bible's claims and contents constitutes an abdication of personal responsibility concerning one's own welfare.

To know that the Bible is reliable is to know that all of what it teaches is reliable. And what it teaches is that the one true God sent His only Son to die for our sins so that we could inherit eternal life as a free gift (John 3:16; Romans 3:22-26). Such a claim is phenomenal in its uniqueness and profundity. If skeptics are given only one reason to objectively examine the claims of the Bible, this alone should be sufficient, because if these claims are true, then God freely offers us more than we could ever imagine. If the Bible is truly God's Word to us, and if we reject its message of salvation, then no other personal decision they make will be more consequential. Therefore no one can fail to ignore the issue of the reliability of the Bible—not merely its historical reliability but its spiritual reliability as well.

We have written this booklet so that Christians will be encouraged in their faith and non-Christians will be challenged to investigate the Bible further—to read it, ponder it, and ultimately to accept it for what it is. Our desire for the reader is expressed in the gratefulness of the apostle Paul to the Thessalonians: "We also thank God continually because, when you received the word of God, which you heard from us, you accepted it not as the word of men, but as it actually is, the word of God, which is at work in you who believe." (1 Thessalonians 2:13 NIV).

In the following pages we will begin by presenting a general defense and proper understanding of the biblical doctrine of inerrancy, the teaching that the Bible is without error. In our second section we will document the accuracy of the Bible textually, historically, and archeologically. In our third section we will examine specific critical arguments about the Bible and show why they are wrong. (A companion volume, *Ready with an Answer*, discusses some of these same topics, and many more, in greater detail.)

Part I
The Primary Issue

1. What is the proper understanding of the biblical doctrine of inerrancy?

If the Bible is inerrant—that is, without error—then it is certainly entirely unique among all the ancient books of the world, whether religious or secular. Given the tens of thousands of details in the Bible that could be either confirmed or disproved by history, archeology, science, etc., and given the fact that

Scripture was written by some 40 authors over a period of 1500 years in many different places and times, to find the Bible without error and in agreement on essentials and particulars is nothing short of striking. In fact, we think something like this can only be explained through divine inspiration. In the pages that follow we will discuss what inerrancy means and what it does not mean. A good general definition of biblical inerrancy is given by Dr. Paul Feinberg:

> Inerrancy means that when all facts are known, the Scriptures in their original autographs and properly interpreted will be shown to be wholly true in everything that they affirm, whether that has to do with doctrine or morality or with the social, physical, or life sciences.[2]

Critics, of course, will immediately point out that we do not have "all the facts" nor do we have the autographs, or original writings, and therefore inerrancy can't be formally proven or rationally defended. While technically it can't be formally proved, inerrancy can certainly be rationally defended. Formal, 100 percent proof is available only in logic and mathematics. For everything else in life, we must base our decisions on degrees of probability. One hundred percent certainty is not available for anything in life, including life itself, so it can hardly be argued that a 99 percent degree of probability for inerrancy is irrelevant. People buy houses, drive cars, and get married taking much higher degrees of risk than this.

Our argument is that preponderance of evidence lies so heavily on the side of inerrancy that it cannot reasonably be doubted, if the evidence is handled fairly. True, we don't have all the facts, but we do have an incredibly large number of them which support inerrancy. And we don't have the autographs, but the manuscript copies which we do possess are collectively autographic for all practical purposes. As we shall see, what all this means is that more than sufficient reason exists for belief in inerrancy. Compared to making other important decisions in life, trusting in the inerrancy of the Bible is one of the easiest to make.

Properly defined, inerrancy must apply "equally to all parts of Scripture as originally written."[3] Thus a belief in what is termed "limited inerrancy"—i.e., inerrancy in doctrine and morals, but errancy in science and history—is impossible to maintain logically because accepting errors in the latter category demands accepting errors in the former category. Why? Because biblical doctrine and morality are inseparably bound to biblical history and science, as we document elsewhere.[4] It is impossible to maintain that the Bible has errors in science and history but is without error in theology and ethics because these categories are logically connected.

For example, if we reject a literal Adam as the first man (Genesis 2:5-7; 1 Corinthians 15:21,45) and his subsequent fall into sin as an error (in deference to the alleged truth of evolution), we must also logically reject as error the declarations of the apostle Paul concerning these beliefs as well as the imputation of Adam's sin to the human race and its consequences (Romans 5:12-19). Further, if Adam and Eve never existed, then Jesus was also in error (Matthew 19:4,5) and biblical Christology and salvation along with Him. Further, if Scripture contains errors in those areas we can test on the basis of historical, archeological, and scientific fact, on what logical basis can we assume it doesn't contain errors in those areas we cannot test, such as theology and ethics (the nature of God, salvation, morality, etc.)?

Finally, the assumption of errancy is self-defeating in another way. Given limited inerrancy, it becomes impossible to tell which Scriptures are inerrant and which are not. The Bible assumes its inerrancy throughout and never even hints that some parts of it are errant. So if Scripture errs, then where does it err and how do we know when, if not even a single error has ever been proven in Scripture? In light of this, one wonders why anyone, especially any Christian, would assume that the Bible contains errors? The real issue is usually that some people think Scripture has errors because it teaches something they don't want to believe, or because it conflicts with some personal theory they think is true but really isn't (e.g., rationalism, scientism, evolution, humanism, feminism, universalism).

But there are other important considerations when we examine the doctrine of inerrancy. To be understood and defended properly, inerrancy must not become subject to certain uncalled for misunderstandings. First, a proper definition of inerrancy does not demand the use of technical language or knowledge of modern science. This would certainly have kept it a closed book to all those without such knowledge. Ongoing scientific precision constantly changes. Such precision for the twentieth century would still not make the Bible correct to the nth degree, for which century's precision should inerrancy reflect—twentieth, twenty-fifth, or thirtieth?

Also, precision may become so precise as to be awkward or useless, practically speaking. To speak of a setting sun is not an error in spite of its scientific imprecision in not referring to the earth's rotation. To cite a biblical example, Jesus said that the mustard seed was "smaller than all other seeds" (Matthew 13:32 NASB). For all we know, humankind has still not discovered the smallest of all seeds. For Jesus a) to have named this seed, or b) to have named the smallest seed currently known to twentieth century botany would, respectively, leave Him a) in possible error through lack of current scientific confirmation or b) actual error by accommodation to limited twentieth century science. In either case, His hearers would either not have understood Him, or questioned His accuracy, or both. Jesus' obvious meaning was that the mustard seed was the smallest of all seeds known to His hearers, which was true, and reflects how the New International Version translates this verse.

Second, everyone knows that it is proper to use general statements about things, so long as they do not contain errors. Inerrancy, for the same reason, does not require strict grammatic, semantic, numeric, or historic precision. For example, September 14, 15, or 16 is correctly referred to as the middle of the month.

Third, inerrancy does not exclude the use of figurative language (e.g., allegory, personification, hyperbole) or various literary genres (apocalyptic, drama, poetry, parable); to exclude these in favor of a wooden literalism would rob Scripture of much of its richness and universal appeal.

Fourth, inerrancy does not demand verbatim exactness when the New Testament quotes the Old, assuming a New Testament quotation does not contradict an Old Testament one. New Testament writers, not to mention the Holy Spirit, had the right to use Old Testament quotations in summary form for purpose of illustration, or other legitimate literary means, just as writers do today.

Fifth, inerrancy does not demand that any given biblical event or account be exhaustively reported.

Sixth, inerrancy assumes the accuracy of what is merely recorded, whether or not it is true (such as accurately recording a lie from Satan [Genesis 3:4] or an incorrect prophecy by a false prophet).

Seventh, inerrancy does not assume the inerrancy of noninspired sources quoted by a biblical writer for purposes of illustration (Acts 17:28). In essence, inerrancy means that the Bible, even though speaking in the common language, never deceives us, never contradicts itself, and can be wholly trusted. Inerrancy means that the Bible is without error.

Having examined what inerrancy does and does not teach, let us now briefly see how this doctrine relates to the nature of divine inspiration and the character of God. Then we will look at the Bible itself to show that it does clearly claim to be inerrant.

Inerrancy is inseparably related to the doctrine of inspiration and the righteous character and infinite power of God. First, the biblical doctrine of inspiration is both verbal and plenary—i.e., involving the very words of Scripture (Matthew 4:4) and extending to every part of Scripture (2 Timothy 3:16). If a righteous and holy God is incapable of inspiring error, then it is logical to conclude that whatever is inspired must be inerrant. Second, the Bible reveals that God is omnipotent—that is, He has absolute power. In other words, He has the means to give His revelation inerrantly.

Thus, if God's inspiration extends to every word of Scripture, then every word of Scripture must be inerrant because of His righteousness. Further, since He is omnipotent He could safeguard the human recipients of inspiration from error, even though His inspiration was given through fallible men.

Thus the Bible either asserts or assumes its own inerrancy from its first book, Genesis, to its last book, Revelation. The term "Thus saith the Lord" or similar expressions are used some 2800 times in the Old Testament (e.g., Jeremiah 1:11; cf. Deuteronomy 18:18; 1 Kings 22:14; Amos 3:1; Exodus 34:27; Jeremiah 36:28; Isaiah 8:20). And in many different ways the Old Testament repeatedly asserts its divine authority. For example, "The grass withers and the flowers fall, but the word of our God stands forever" (Isaiah 40:8 NIV). In brief, the Old Testament is either God's Word or a monumental fraud. Inspiration (or inerrancy) is explicitly asserted for 68 percent of the Old Testament (26 of 39 books). The remaining books have either an implicit claim or a characteristic quality which serves for such an implicit claim. (Where explicit claim is lacking, particular reasons may exist for this.[5]) New Testament assertions to the verbal, plenary inspiration of the Old Testament provides additional corroboration. Thus, "Twenty of twenty-two Old Testament books (or 90 percent) have their authority and/or authenticity directly affirmed by the New Testament."[6] As we discuss more fully later, particularly relevant are the declarations of Jesus who was God incarnate (Jn. 1:1; 5:46; 8:14-16; 26, 28; 12:48-50; 14:6; 2 Pet. 1:20; Phil. 2:1-8; Titus 2:13). As God incarnate, Jesus was incapable of teaching error (John 12:48-50; Matthew 24:35). In John 17:17 NASB Jesus said, "Thy Word is truth" and in Matthew 4:4,"Man shall not live on bread alone, but on every word that proceeds out of the mouth of God" (NASB). In both instances He could only have referred to the complete Old Testament canon of the Jews then extant (Luke 24:27). This affirms 100 percent of the Old Testament as inspired and therefore inerrant.

As Drs. Geisler and Nix correctly point out, "Christ is the key to the inspiration and canonization of the Scriptures."[7] Jesus not only confirmed the entire Old Testament as inspired, He preauthenticated the inspiration (i.e., inerrancy) of the New Testament. Because of Christ's promise to the disciples that the Holy Spirit "will teach you all things and will remind you of everything I have said to you" (John 14:26 NIV; referring e.g., to the Gospels, cf. Matthew 24:35) and that the Holy Spirit "will guide you into all truth" (John 16:13 NIV; cf. vv. 14, 15, referring e.g., to the remainder of the New Testament), it is not surprising that "virtually every New Testament writer claimed that his writing was divinely authoritative. . . . The cumulative effect of this self-testimony is an overwhelming confirmation that the New Testament writers claimed inspiration."[8] Some examples of claims for the inspiration (i.e., inerrancy) of the prophetic New Testament include 2 Timothy 3:16; 2 Peter 1:20,21; 3:2, 16, Revelation 1:1-3; 22:18,9, 1 Thessalonians 4:8. Indeed, the fact that virtually every New Testament writer assumed his writing was as binding and authoritative as the Old Testament asserts a great deal, for such writers were Orthodox Jews who believed that God's word was heretofore confined to the accepted Old Testament canon. To add to it was a horrible presumption unless divine inspiration were clearly present. However, the very fact of the arrival of the prophesied new covenant (predicted in Jeremiah, Ezekiel, etc.), coupled with the incarnation and atonement of Jesus, required a corresponding body of divine revelation to explain and expound these events, just as was true for the activity of God in the old covenant. There can be no doubt that the Bible teaches its own inerrancy. (In *Ready with an Answer* we show how strong the scriptural testimony is.)

Skeptics, however, reject inerrancy because of the unsupported presuppositions they bring to Scripture. Critics generally assume that miracles are impossible by definition, the unstated corollary being that God doesn't exist either. But how do they know this with absolute assurance—by infallible knowledge? If many or most of the greatest minds throughout history and today have believed that God exists, how do critics safely assume otherwise? Modern scientific rationalism has explained very little of the heights and depths of the universe. To declare absolutely that God does not exist and that inerrant inspiration is impossible is itself impossible to maintain logically unless one is God and has the omniscience to be absolutely certain of the impossibility. It is merely presumption to assume that an infinite, personal God could never communicate His revelation inerrantly.

Besides, sufficient evidence exists to show that the Bible is divinely inspired. For example, the presence of supernatural prophecy about the future cannot be denied except on the basis of an antisupernatural bias. Thus the internal and external evidence clearly supports a pre-neo-Babylonian composition for Isaiah and a neo-Babylonian composition for Daniel.[9] Yet Isaiah predicts, for example, King Cyrus by name long before he lived (44:28-45:6), and the nature, person, mission, and death of the Jewish Messiah (e.g., 9:6; 53:1-12). Similarly, the prophet Daniel (Matthew 24:15) predicts the Medo-Persian, Greek, and Roman empires so clearly that antisupernaturalists are forced, against all the evidence, to date his book at 165 B.C. and thus imply that it is a forgery (Daniel chapters 2 and 7; cf. 11:1-35 in light of subsequent Persian and Greek history and the dynasties of the Egyptians and Syrians).[10] First Kings 13:1,2 predicts King Josiah 300 years before he was born and Micah 5:2 predicts the very birthplace of Jesus 700 years before He was born. How are we to account for such things if the Bible is not a divine book?

Finally, the person and resurrection of Jesus Christ proves the inerrancy of Scripture, for if Jesus rose from the dead—and this must be accepted as a fact of history[11]—then His claims about Himself must be true. If so, then He must be God incarnate (John 5:18, 21-26; 1:30-38; 11:4, 25; 14:9), and thus His teaching on an inerrant Scripture must be accepted—unless we are to suppose that God lies or contradicts Himself, which He Himself denies (Hebrews 6:18; Titus 1:2; 2 Timothy 2:13; Numbers 23:19). Indeed, when even a noted Jewish scholar of the New Testament who rejects Jesus' Messiahship accepts His bodily resurrection "as a historical event" and "a fact of history" we can be certain that the resurrection is at least worth even the critics' impartial investigation.[12]

Following Montgomery and Sproul,[13] a logical defense of inerrancy may be constructed based on Christ's resurrection:

1. On the basis of accepted principles of historic and textual analysis the New Testament documents are shown to be reliable and trustworthy historical documents. That is, they give accurate primary source evidence for the life and death of Jesus Christ. (See Question 2.)

2. In the Gospel records, Jesus claimed to be God incarnate (John 5:18; 10:27-33). He exercised numerable divine prerogatives, and rested his claims on His numerous and abundantly testified, historically unparalleled miracles (John 10:37,38) and His forthcoming physical resurrection from the dead (John 10:17,18).

3. In each Gospel, Christ's resurrection is minutely described, and for 2000 years it has been incapable of disproof despite the detailed scholarship of the world's best skeptics. The simple truth is that the historic fact of the resurrection of Christ proves His claim to deity (Romans 1:3,4). The resurrection cannot be rejected a priori on antisupernaturalist grounds, for miracles are impossible only if so defined. The probability of a miracle is determined by the cumulative weight of the evidence, and not on philosophical bias.

4. Because Jesus is the Son of God, He is an infallible authority. In this role He taught that Scripture originates from a holy God and is inerrant, since that which originates from an utterly trustworthy God must be utterly trustworthy itself (cf. John Wenham, *Christ and the Bible*).

Our conclusion is that both the claims and the miraculous nature of the Bible, which speak for its inspiration and inerrancy, as well as the infallible pronouncements of God incarnate on an inerrant Scripture, are sufficient reason to accept the proposition that the Bible is inerrant. In our next seven questions we will see how the facts surrounding the biblical text and content support inerrancy and biblical authority.

Part 2
The Accuracy of the Biblical Text

2. What can a military historian tell us about the reliability of the New Testament?*

Christians and skeptical non-Christians have different views about the credibility of the Gospels and the rest of the New Testament. For the Christian, nothing is more vital than the very words of Jesus Himself who promised, "Heaven and earth will pass away, but my words will never pass away" (Matthew 24:35 NIV). Jesus' promise is of vital importance. In other words, if His words were not accurately recorded in the Gospels, how can anyone know what He really taught? The truth is that we couldn't know. Further, if the remainder of the New Testament cannot be established as historically

---

* A more through treatment is found in our *Ready with an Answer* (Harvest House, 1997).

reliable, then little can be known about what true Christianity really is, teaches, or means. Who is right in this debate—the Christians, who claim that the New Testament is historically accurate, or the critics of the New Testament, who claim otherwise?

The conservative view of Scripture maintains that, on the basis of accepted bibliographic, internal, external, and other criteria, the New Testament text can be established as reliable history in spite of the novel and sometimes ingenious speculations of critics, who, while often familiar with the facts, refuse to accept them due to a preexisting bias. Textually, we have restored over 99 percent of the autographs and there is simply no legitimate basis upon which to doubt the credibility and accuracy of the New Testament writers. Further, the methods used by the critics (such as form and redaction criticism methods) have been weighed in the balance of even secular scholarship and been found wanting. Their use in biblical analysis is therefore unjustified. Even in a positive sense, the fruit they have born is minuscule, while negatively they are responsible for a tremendous weight of destruction in people's confusion over biblical authority and their confidence in the Bible (see also our *Facts on False Views of Jesus*).

In this sense the critics conform to the warnings of Chauncey Sanders, Associate Professor of Military History, The Air University, Maxwell Air Force Base, Montgomery, Alabama. In his *Introduction to Research in English Literary History*, he warns literary critics to be certain that they are also careful to examine the evidence against their case: "He must be as careful to collect evidence against his theory as for it. It may go against the grain to be very assiduous in searching for ammunition to destroy one's own case; but it must be remembered that the overlooking of a single detail may be fatal to one's whole argument. Moreover, it is the business of the scholar to seek the truth, and the satisfaction of having found it should be ample recompense for having to give up a cherished but untenable theory."[14]

In order to resolve this issue of New Testament reliability, the following ten facts cannot logically be denied.

Fact One: The Bibliographical Test (corroboration from textual transmission)

The historical accuracy of the New Testament can be proven by subjecting it to three generally accepted tests for determining historical reliability. Such tests are used in literary criticism and the study of historical documents in general.

(These are discussed by Sanders in his *Introduction to Research in English Literary History*.)[15] These involve 1) bibliographical, 2) internal, and 3) external examinations of the text and other evidence.

The bibliographical test seeks to determine whether or not we can reconstruct the original manuscript from the extant copies. For the New Testament we have 5300 Greek manuscripts and manuscript portions, 10,000 Latin Vulgate and 9300 other versions, and 36,000 early (100–300 A.D.) patristic quotations of the New Testament. All but a few verses of the entire New Testament could be reconstructed from these alone.[16] What does this mean?

Few scholars question the general reliability of ancient classical literature on the basis of the manuscripts we possess. Yet this collection is vastly inferior to that of the New Testament. For example, of 16 well-known classical authors (e.g., Plutarch, Tacitus, Sentonius, Polybius, Thucydides, Xenophon, etc.), the total number of extant copies is typically less than ten and the earliest copies date from 750 to 1600 years after the original manuscript was first penned).[17]

We need only compare such slim evidence to the mass of biblical documentation involving over 24,000 manuscript portions, manuscripts, and versions, the earliest fragment and complete copies dating between only 50 and 300 years after originally written.

Given the fact that the early Greek manuscripts (the papyri and early uncials) date much closer to the originals than for any other ancient literature; and given the overwhelming additional abundance of manuscript attestation, any doubt as to the integrity or authenticity of the New Testament text has been removed no matter what any critic claims. Indeed, this kind of evidence supplied by the New Testament (both amount and quality) is the dream of the historian. No other ancient literature has ever come close to supplying historians and textual critics with such an abundance of data.

Dr. F. F. Bruce, former Rylands Professor of Biblical Criticism and Exegesis at the University of Manchester, asserts of the New Testament: "There is no body of ancient literature in the world which enjoys such a wealth of good textual attestation as the New Testament."[18] Professor Bruce further comments, "The evidence for our New Testament writings is ever so much greater than the evidence for many writings of classical writers, the authenticity of which no one dreams of questioning. And if the New Testament were a collection of secular writings, their authenticity would generally be regarded as beyond all doubt."[19]

It is this wealth of material that has enabled scholars such as Westcott and Hort, Ezra Abbott, Philip Schaff, A. T. Robertson, Norman Geisler, and William Nix to place the restoration of the original text at 99 percent plus.[20] No other document of the ancient period is as accurately preserved as the New Testament:

> Hort's estimate of "substantial variation" for the New Testament is one-tenth of 1 percent; Abbot's estimate is one-fourth of 1 percent; and even Hort's figure including trivial variation is less than 2 percent. Sir Frederic Kenyon well summarizes the situation:

> The number of manuscripts of the New Testament . . . is so large that it is practically certain that the true reading of every doubtful passage is preserved in some one or another of these ancient authorities. This can be said of no other ancient book in the world.

> Scholars are satisfied that they possess substantially the true text of the principal Greek and Roman writers whose works have come down to us, of Sophocles, of Thucydides, of Cicero, of Virgil; yet our knowledge depends on a mere handful of manuscripts, whereas the manuscripts of the New Testament are counted by hundreds and even thousands.[21]

In other words, those who question the reliability of the New Testament must also question the reliability of virtually every ancient writing the world possesses! So how can the New Testament be rejected when its documentation is 100 times that of other ancient literature? If it is impossible to question the world's ancient classics, it is far more impossible to question the New Testament.[22]

In addition, none of the established New Testament canon is lost or missing, not even a verse, as indicated by variant readings. The New Testament, then, passes the bibliographical test and must, by far, be graded with the highest mark of any ancient literature.

Fact Two: The Internal Evidence Test (corroboration from content accuracy)

This test asserts that one is to assume the truthful reporting of an ancient document (and not assume either fraud, incompetence, or error) unless the author of the document has disqualified himself by their presence. For example, do the

New Testament writers contradict themselves? Is there anything in their writing which causes one to objectively suspect their trustworthiness?

The answer is no. There is lack of proven fraud or error on the part of any New Testament writer. Instead, there is evidence of careful eyewitness reporting throughout the New Testament. The caution exercised by the writers, their personal conviction that what they wrote was true, and the lack of demonstrable error or contradiction indicate that the Gospel authors (and indeed all the New Testament authors) pass the second test as well (Luke 1:1-4; John 19:35; 21:24; Acts 1:1-3; 2:22; 26:24-26; 2 Peter 1:16; 1 John 1:1-3).

For example, the kinds of things the Gospel writers include in their narratives offers strong evidence for their integrity. They record their own sins and failures, even serious ones (Matthew 26:56, 69-75; Mark 10:35-45). They do not hesitate from recording accurately even the most difficult and consequential statements of Jesus (John 6:41-71). They forthrightly supply the embarrassing and even capital charges of Jesus' own enemies. Thus, even though Jesus was their very Messiah and Lord, they not only record the charges that Jesus broke the Sabbath, but that He was 1) born in fornication, 2) a blasphemer and a liar, 3) insane, and 4) demonized (Matthew 1:19, 25; John 8:41; Matthew 26:65; John 7:20; 8:48, 52; 10:20, 33; etc.).

To encounter such honesty in reporting incidents of this nature gives one assurance that the Gospel writers placed a very high premium on truthfulness.

Fact Three: The External Evidence Test (corroboration from reliable sources outside the New Testament)

This test seeks to either corroborate or falsify the documents on the basis of additional historical literature and data. (In this section we will look at Christian sources; in the next section non-Christian sources.) Is there corroborating evidence for the claims made in the New Testament outside the New Testament? Or are the claims or events of the New Testament successfully refuted by other competent reports or eyewitnesses? Are there statements or assertions in the New Testament which are demonstrably false according to known archeological, historic, scientific, or other data?

The New Testament again passes the test. For example, Luke's careful historical writing has been documented from detailed, personal, archeological investigation by former critic Sir William Ramsay, who stated after his painstaking research, "Luke's history is unsurpassed in respect of its trustworthiness."[23] A. N. Sherwin-White, the distinguished historian of Rome, stated of Luke: "For [the book of] Acts the confirmation of historicity is overwhelming. Any attempt to reject its basic historicity even in matters of detail must now appear absurd."[24]

Papias, a student of the apostle John[25] and Bishop of Hierapolis, around 130 A.D. observed that the apostle John himself noted that the apostle Mark in writing his Gospel "wrote down accurately . . . whatsoever he [Peter] remembered of the things said or done by Christ. Mark committed no error . . . for he was careful of one thing, not to omit any of the things he [Peter] had heard, and not to state any of them falsely."[26]

Further, fragments of Papias' Exposition of the Oracles of the Lord, ca. 140 A.D. (III, XIX, XX) assert that the Gospels of Matthew, Mark, and John are all based on reliable eyewitness testimony (his portion on Luke is missing).[27]

Even 200 years of scholarly rationalistic biblical criticism (such as form, source, and redaction approaches) have proven nothing except that the writers were careful and honest reporters of the events recorded and that these methods attempting to discredit them were flawed and biased from the start.

Fact Four: Corroboration from Non-Christian Sources

The existence of both Jewish and secular accounts to a significant degree confirm the picture of Christ that we have in the New Testament. Scholarly research such as that by Dr. Gary R. Habermas in *Ancient Evidence for the Life of Jesus* and other texts indicates that "a broad outline of the life of Jesus" and His death by crucifixion can be reasonably and directly inferred from entirely non-Christian sources.[28] For example, concerning Jesus' death by crucifixion and resurrection from the dead:

> Using only the information gleaned from these ancient extrabiblical sources, what can we conclude concerning the death and resurrection of Jesus? Can these events be historically established based on these sources alone? Of the seventeen documents examined in this chapter, eleven different works speak of the death of Jesus in varying amounts of detail, with five of these specifying crucifixion as the mode. When these sources are examined by normal historical procedures used with other ancient documents, the result is conclusive.

It is this author's view that the death of Jesus by crucifixion can be asserted as a historical fact from this
data. . . .[29]

Further, he points out that the resurrection of Christ itself
can be indirectly inferred from non-Christian sources.[30]

Fact Five: Corroboration from Archeology

There exists detailed archeological confirmation for the
New Testament documents.[31] (See Question 3.) As archeologist
Dr. Clifford Wilson, author of New Light on the New Testament
Letters; New Light on the Gospels; Rock, Relics and Biblical
Reliability; and a 17-volume set on the archeological confirma-
tion of the Bible, writes: "Those who know the facts now
recognize that the New Testament must be accepted as a
remarkably accurate source book."[32]

Fact Six: Corroboration from Enemies' Silence

The complete inability of the numerous enemies of Jesus
and the early church to discredit early Christian claims (when
they had both the motive and the ability to do so) argues
strongly for their veracity in light of the stupendous nature of
those claims (e.g., Christ's messiahship and resurrection) and
the relative ease of disproof (Jesus' failure to fulfill prophecy;
producing Jesus' body).

Fact Seven: Corroboration from Eyewitnesses

The presence of hundreds of eyewitnesses to the events
recorded in the New Testament[33] would surely have prohibited
any alteration or distortion of the facts, just as today any false
reporting as to the events of the Vietnam War or World War II
would be immediately corrected on the basis of living eyewitnesses and historic records.

Some argue that the Gospel writers' reporting of miracles
can't be trusted because they were only giving their religiously
excited "subjective experience" of Jesus, not objectively
reporting real miraculous events. They thought Jesus did miracles, but were mistaken.

What is ignored by critics is what the text plainly states and
the fact that the Gospel writers could not have gotten away with
such a deception in their own day. They claimed that these
things were done openly, not in a corner (Acts 26:26)—that they
were literally eyewitnesses of the miraculous nature and deeds
of Jesus (Luke 1:2; Acts 2:32; 4:20; 2 Peter 1:16) and that their

testimony should be believed because it was true (John 20:30,31; 21:24).

Indeed, they wrote that Jesus Himself presented His miracles in support of His own claims to be both the prophesied Messiah and God incarnate. In Mark 2:8-11, when He healed the paralytic, He did so "that you may know that the Son of Man has authority on earth to forgive sins"(NIV)—a clear claim to being God. In John 10:33, when the Jews accused Jesus of blaspheming because as supposedly only a man He was claiming to be God, what was Jesus' response? "Do not believe me unless I do what my Father does. But if I do it, even though you do not believe me, believe the miracles, that you may learn and understand that the Father is in me, and I in the Father" (John 10:37,38 NIV). This is clearly another claim to deity. When John the Baptist was in jail and apparently had doubts as to whether or not Jesus was the Messiah—after all, if Jesus was the Messiah, John probably reasoned, he should not be in jail—what did Jesus do? He told John's disciples to go and report about the miracles that Jesus did which were in fulfillment of specific messianic prophecy (Matthew 11:2-5). Many other examples could be added.

The truth is that the teachings and miracles of Jesus, as any independent reading of the Gospels will prove, are so inexorably bound together that if one removes the miracles one must also discard the teachings, and vice versa. It is logically impossible to have any other Jesus than the biblical one. But it is precisely the biblical Jesus—His deeds and teachings—which have such abundant eyewitness testimony, as any reading of the Gospels and Acts proves.

Fact Eight: Corroboration from Date of Authorship

The fact that both conservatives (e.g., F. F. Bruce, John Wenham) and liberals (Bishop John A. T. Robinson) have penned defenses of early dating for the New Testament is a witness to the strength of the data for an early date. For example, in *Redating Matthew, Mark and Luke,* noted conservative British scholar John Wenham presents a convincing argument that the synoptic Gospels are to be dated before 55 A.D. He dates Matthew at 40 A.D. (some tradition says the early 30s); Mark at 45 A.D.; and Luke no later than 51-55 A.D.[34]

Even liberal bishop John A. T. Robinson argued in his *Redating the New Testament* that the entire New Testament was written and in circulation between 40 and 65 A.D.[35] And liberal Peter Stuhlmacher of Tubingen, trained in Bultmann's critical methodology of form criticism, says, "As a Western scripture scholar, I am inclined to doubt these [Gospel] stories, but as a historian, I am obligated to take them as reliable." And, "The biblical texts as they stand are the best hypothesis we have until now to explain what really happened."[36]

Indeed, even to some critical scholars, it is becoming an increasingly persuasive argument that all the New Testament books were written before 70 A.D.—within a single generation of the death of Christ, and perhaps earlier.

The implications of this are weighty. A New Testament written before 70 A.D. virtually destroys the edifice on which higher-critical premises regarding the New Testament are based, for insufficient time now remains for members of the early church to have embellished the records with their own particularist views. What the New Testament reports, it reports accurately.

Fact Nine: Corroboration from Critical Methods Themselves

Even critical methods indirectly support New Testament reliability. Although higher-critical theories in general reject biblical reliability a priori, when such theories "are subjected to the same analytical scrutiny as they apply to the New Testament documents they will be found to make their own contribution to validating the historicity of those records."[37]

Fact Ten: Confirmation from Legal Testimony and Skeptics

Finally, we must also concede the historicity of the New Testament when we consider the fact that many great minds of legal history have, on the grounds of strict legal evidence alone, accepted the New Testament as reliable history—not to mention the fact that many brilliant, skeptical intellects of history and today have converted to Christianity on the basis of the historical evidence (Saul of Tarsus, Athanagoras, Augustine, George Lyttleton, Gilbert West, C. S. Lewis, Frank Morison, Sir William Ramsay, John Warwick Montgomery, etc.).

Lawyers, of course, are expertly trained in the matter of evaluating evidence and are perhaps the most qualified in the task of weighing data critically. Is it any coincidence that so many of them throughout history have concluded in favor of the truth of the Christian Scriptures?

What of the "father of international law," Hugo Grotius, who wrote *The Truth of the Christian Religion* (1627)? Or the greatest authority in English and American common-law evidence in the nineteenth century, Harvard Law School Professor Simon Greenleaf, who wrote *Testimony of the Evangelists* in which he powerfully demonstrated the reliability of the

Gospels?[38] What of Edmund H. Bennett (1824–1898), for over 20 years the Dean of Boston University Law School, who penned *The Four Gospels from a Lawyer's Standpoint* (1899)?[39] What of Irwin Linton, who in his time had represented cases before the Supreme Court and wrote *A Lawyer Examines the Bible*, in which he stated:

> So invariable had been my observation that he who does not accept wholeheartedly the evangelical, conservative belief in Christ and the Scriptures has never read, has forgotten, or never been able to weigh—and certainly is utterly unable to refute—the irresistible force of the cumulative evidence upon which such faith rests, that there seems ample ground for the conclusion that such ignorance is an invariable element in such unbelief. And this is so even though the unbeliever be a preacher, who is supposed to know this subject if he know no other.[40]

What of hundreds of contemporary lawyers who, on the grounds of strict legal evidence, accept the New Testament as historically reliable? We must emphasize that to reject the New Testament accounts as true history is, by definition, to reject the canons of legitimate historical study. If this cannot be done, the New Testament must be retained as careful historical reporting.

The New Testament has proven itself reliable in the crucible of history. It is the New Testament critic who has been unable to prove his case. Nor are the implications small. Legal scholar J. N. D. Anderson observes in *Christianity: The Witness of History*:

> . . . it seems to me inescapable that anyone who chanced to read the pages of the New Testament for the first time would come away with one overwhelming impression— that here is a faith firmly rooted in certain allegedly historical events, a faith which would be false and mis- leading if those events had not actually taken place, but which, if they did take place, is unique in its relevance and exclusive in its demands on our allegiance. For these events did not merely set a "process in motion and then themselves sink back into the past. The unique historical origin of Christianity is ascribed permanent, authorita- tive, absolute significance; what happened once is said to have happened once for all and therefore to have contin- uous efficacy."[41]

22

3. What truth have the stones cried out concerning 4000 years of biblical history?*

Recently there has been much interest in biblical archeology among Christians whose attention to archeology is primarily apologetic—i.e., how it confirms the biblical record. Such confirmation is hardly surprising to the one who knows that the Bible is the inerrant Word of God, but it has been an unexpected occurrence to those who have believed that the Bible is merely the record of fallible men. Such critics had expected that archeology would disprove Christian claims in many areas.

In what way does archeology confirm the biblical record? Primarily by demonstrating that it is trustworthy where it can be tested. Obviously, archeological data is still relatively sparse and biblical claims cannot be tested everywhere, so archeology can hardly be expected to confirm every statement of biblical history, geography, culture, etc. What we do have is the knowledge that there are no final problems because the Scriptures are the inerrant Word of God.

The significant point is this: When sufficient factual information becomes known and is properly interpreted, *it always confirms the biblical record*. In cases where a discovery initially seems not to confirm the Bible, sufficient factual data is never encountered in order to disprove a biblical statement. Given the thousands of minute details in the Bible that archeology has the opportunity to disprove, this confirmation of the biblical record is absolutely striking. As scientist and Christian apologist Dr. Henry M. Morris points out, "It must be extremely significant that, in view of the great mass of corroborative evidence regarding the biblical history of these periods, there exists today not one unquestionable find of archeology that proves the Bible to be in error at any point."[42]

Dr. Clifford Wilson ends Volume 17 of his series of volumes that survey the archeological confirmation of the Bible by concluding that "it is remarkable that where confirmation is possible and has come to light, the Bible stands investigation in ways that are unique in all literature. Its superiority to attack, its capacity to withstand criticism, its amazing facility to be proved right after all, are all staggering by any standards of scholarship. Seemingly assured results 'disproving' the Bible have a habit of backfiring. Over and over again the Bible has been vindicated. That is true from Genesis to Revelation, as we have seen in this book."[43]

---

* A more thorough treatment is found in our *Ready with an Answer* (Harvest House, 1997).

In essence, from the perspective of the hope of biblical critics—if that hope was to be proved correct—archeological research has provided vast opportunities to establish their critical view of the Bible. Their belief was that the Bible merely constituted the error-filled writings of men, and was of no particular or lasting spiritual importance. But their hopes have consistently been smashed, for the Bible has stood up to the investigation of a type that has not been hurled at any other book of history.

In conclusion, we need to remind ourselves of the spiritual implications of biblical archeology: "The serious investigator has every reason for great confidence in the reliability of both Old and New Testament Scriptures.... However, the historical material—seen through archeology to be of remarkable integrity—is penned by the same men who witnessed and recorded the miracles and elaborated on spiritual realities. It is reasonable to believe that they would be as reliable in those areas as they are in the areas now subject to investigation by archeology."[44]

Part 3
Dealing with Critical Views

4. Are critics correct in maintaining that the "assured results" of higher criticism have discredited biblical reliability?

Modern critics typically appeal to the "assured results" of rationalistic methods of higher criticism (e.g., source, form, redaction criticism) to "prove" that the Bible isn't inerrant. As the 74 members of the so-called "Jesus Seminar" wrote, "The public is poorly informed of the assured results of critical scholarship, although those results are commonly taught in colleges, universities, and seminaries."[45] Here the assumption is that the investigative methodology used by the critics has proven there are errors in the Bible. However, as we thoroughly documented in *The Facts on False Views of Jesus*, when the critics speak of "assured results" they are being presumptuous. The mere fact that a majority of modern liberal, rationalistic theologians accept higher criticism is hardly a guarantee that such a methodology is either impartial or legitimate. To rule "solely on the basis of the assured results of higher criticism" is unwise if such results are in fact anything but assured. The truth is that higher criticism and its methodology have proven themselves almost worthless. Far from proving an error in Scripture, they have only served by default to bolster the claim to the inspiration and inerrancy of the Bible. Let's see why.

The historical criticism of the skeptics suffers from the same conceptual illness as rationalistic antisupernaturalism. It assumes that the Bible is not divinely inspired, but was written by fallible men with personal agendas to uphold, and therefore has errors. If one assumes error, one can usually "find" error, whether or not the conclusion is justified (i.e., whether or not other possible explanations exist which are consistent with a position of inerrancy). What critics are unwilling to accept is that the last 200 years of intense critical study have never proven an error in the Bible. With millions of man-hours expended, this should be considered a most remarkable confirmation of biblical inerrancy. Thus it is the position of the *higher critics who doubt Scripture* that has been repeatedly overturned, and not that of the conservative Christian who upholds inerrancy

Consider the conclusions of several scholars with impeccable academic credentials. Men having such encyclopedic knowledge could hardly have made the statements below and have them successfully gone unchallenged unless such statements were true.

Dr. John Warwick Montgomery graduated from Cornell University with distinction in philosophy, Phi Beta Kappa. Then he went on to earn the Ph.D. from the University of Chicago, a second doctorate in theology from the University of Strasborg, France, and seven additional graduate degrees in theology, law, library science, and other fields. He has written over 125 scholarly journal articles, plus 40 books, many of them defending Christian faith against skeptical views. He has held numerous prestigious appointments, is a founding member of the World Association of Law Professors and a member of the American Society of International Law, and is honored in *Who's Who in America, Who's Who in American Law, The Directory of American Scholars, International Scholars Directory, Who's Who in France, Who's Who in Europe,* and *Who's Who in the World.* Men with the kind of background, temperament, and philosophical premises such as Dr. Montgomery simply do not believe in Christianity apart from sufficient evidence. Dr. Montgomery asserts as to alleged biblical contradictions, a favorite of the critics: "I myself have never encountered an alleged contradiction in the Bible which could not be cleared up by the use of the original languages of the Scriptures and/or by the use of accepted principles of literary and historical interpretation."[46]

Dr. Gleason L. Archer was an undergraduate classics major who received training in Latin, Greek, French, and German at Harvard University. At seminary he majored in Hebrew, Aramaic, and Arabic, and in postgraduate study he became involved with Akkadian and Syriac, teaching courses on these subjects. He has had a special interest in Middle Kingdom Egyptian studies, and at the Oriental Institute in Chicago he did specialized study in Eighteenth Dynasty historical records as well as studying Coptic and Sumerian. In addition, he obtained a full law degree and was admitted to the Massachusetts Bar. He has also visited the Holy Land, where he personally inspected most of the important archeological sites and spent time in Beirut, Lebanon, for a specialized study of modern literary Arabic. He holds the B.D. from Princeton Theological Seminary and the Ph.D. from Harvard Graduate School.

This background enabled Dr. Archer to become an expert in the issue of charges of alleged errors and contradictions in Scripture:

> In my opinion this charge can be refuted and its falsity exposed by an objective study done in a consistent, evangelical perspective. . . . I candidly believe I have been confronted with just about all the biblical difficulties under discussion in theological circles today—especially those pertaining to the interpretation and defense of Scripture. . . . As I have dealt with one apparent discrepancy after another and have studied the alleged contradictions between the biblical record and the evidence of linguistics, archeology, or science, my confidence in the trustworthiness of Scripture has been repeatedly verified and strengthened by the discovery that almost every problem in Scripture that has ever been discovered by man, from ancient times until now, has been dealt with in a completely satisfactory manner by the biblical text itself—or else by objective archeological information.[47]

Given the fact that Dr. Archer has graduated from Princeton and Harvard, has done extensive studies in archeology and other areas, has become fluent in 15 languages, and has received full training in legal evidences, the above statement can hardly be summarily dismissed by critics.

But there are many similar testimonies by other renowned scholars. Dr. Robert Dick Wilson (Ph.D., Princeton), an Old Testament authority and author of *A Scientific Investigation of the Old Testament,* could read the New Testament in nine different languages by the age of 25. In addition, he could repeat from memory a Hebrew translation of the entire New Testament without missing a single syllable and do the same with large portions of the Old Testament. He proceeded to learn 45 languages and dialects and was also a master of paleography and philology: "I have made it an invariable habit never to accept an objection to a statement of the Old Testament without subjecting it to a most thorough investigation, linguistically and factually" and "I defy any man to make an attack upon the Old Testament on the grounds of evidence that I cannot investigate." His conclusion was that no critic has ever succeeded in proving an error in the Old Testament.[48]

Rev. John W. Haley examined 900 alleged problems in Scripture, concluding, "I cannot but avow, as the [conclusion] of my investigation, the profound conviction that *every difficulty and discrepancy in the scriptures is . . . capable of a fair and reasonable solution."*[49] Dr. William Arndt of the standard Arndt and Gingrich Lexicon concluded in his own study of alleged contradictions and errors in the Bible, "We may say with full conviction that no instances of this sort occur anywhere in the Scriptures."[50]

Despite such testimony, the negative conclusions of higher criticism do underscore a key element in this discussion: that of how we should approach Scripture. Should we approach it with a trust of its claim to inerrancy—a claim based on solid evidence in support of it—or with a distrust which seeks to harmonize the data with our own negative presuppositions? As one scholar observed, "The truth is that most scholars end up with conclusions remarkably similar to the presuppositions with which they began their study."[51] Indeed, if the very basis for every higher critical method is predicated upon "alien and unjustified philosophical presuppositions,"[52] is a person truly being objective and fair in his treatment of the biblical text when utilizing such methods, especially when "higher criticism ends up rejecting the truth of the biblical content it is supposed to clarify"? Higher criticism is not neutral; it begins with a negative and unjustified presupposition of errancy which flies in the face of facts. How then can its results be "assured"?

Presuppositions are not proven facts, and the philosophical, historical, or scientific assumptions underlying higher criticism are far from sound in themselves.[53]

Put another way, once one is at least willing to believe that Scripture may be inerrant, he should be logically forced to accept Jesus' view of Scripture as inerrant on the basis of Jesus' divine nature and verifiably accurate Gospel teachings. The critic who is unwilling to believe inerrancy unless it is 100 percent "proven" can never believe it because the state of human knowledge will always be less than 100 percent. It seems only fair that, given the phenomena of Scripture in general, including its claims to inspiration and inerrancy, fulfilled prophecy, archeological confirmation, accuracy in textual transmission, etc., the biblical text should be considered innocent until proven guilty. Further, no critical methodology can be considered legitimate by Christians if it questions the reliability of what God has clearly spoken. If men are presumed innocent until proven guilty, how is it we assume that God is guilty until we prove Him innocent?

The conclusion is that someone must be the judge of Scripture. Either it must be God who has already borne witness to its authority and inerrancy (Isaiah 40:8; John 10:34; 5:46,47), or it must be human beings, who judge God to be in error. What an unfortunate situation the critics' assumptions force them to! Critics must assume error where Jesus declares truth; they must assert the superiority of finite and fallen human reason above divine revelation. In essence, they must make an idol of their own minds, for in that they establish an authoritative criterion above that of God Himself, they commit a form of idolatry.

God has left us no alternative: If we do not accept Him at His word, we are left with precious little. Dr. J. I. Packer is correct when he writes:

> Liberal theology, in its pride, has long insisted that we are wiser than our fathers about the Bible, and must not read it as they did, but must base our approach to it on the "assured results" of criticism, making due allowances for the human imperfections and errors of its authors. This insistence has a threefold effect. (1) It produces a new papalism—the infallibility of the scholars, from whom we learn what the "assured results" are. (2) It raises a doubt about every single Bible passage, as to whether it truly embodies revelation or not. (3) And it destroys the reverent, receptive, self-distrusting attitude of approach to the Bible, without which it cannot be known to be "God's Word written." . . . The result? The spiritual famine of which Amos spoke. God judges our pride by leaving us to the barrenness, hunger, and discomfort which flow from our self-induced inability to hear His Word.[54]

Dr. Harold Lindsell comments on the complications of the critics' claim that no one can really understand the Bible apart from accepting the legitimacy of the critics' "findings":

> Worst of all, and this must be said again and again, it makes the Bible a closed book to the common man. He cannot read it and know what it means if the historical-critical conclusions are correct. No ordinary reader of the Bible could possibly come to this conclusion simply by reading it. The conclusion the common reader would draw would be antithetical to those of the higher critic. Also, the evangelical faith itself is mistaken if the historical-critical methodology is correct.[55]

Unfortunately, portions of evangelicalism itself are now infected. In adopting higher critical methods, some evangelicals are accepting the premise that man can profitably sit in skeptical judgment on the Bible, God's Word. We seriously doubt that these evangelicals would ever have considered that Jesus did not say the things He did had they never been exposed to something like redaction criticism. If one casts doubt on Jesus' own words, or the authenticity of Daniel and Isaiah, or the historicity of Adam and Eve or Jonah, when the biblical and historical data are conclusively in their favor, one certainly no longer trusts wholly in God's Word.

In the end, we are forced to agree with Dr. Montgomery that the conclusions of higher criticism are far from assured; they are in fact unworthy of our trust:

> I have pointed out again and again that such "assured results" are nonexistent, that redaction criticism, documentary criticism, and historical-critical method have been weighed in the balance of secular scholarship and found wanting, and that the burden of proof remains on those who want to justify these subjectivistic methods, not on those who take historical documents at face value when their primary-source character can be established by objective determination of authorship and date.[56]

Thus to adopt a conclusion about the errancy of the biblical text on the basis of the discredited methodology of higher criticism is not only highly suspect, it is entirely unfounded.

5. Doesn't everyone see things differently?

We have stated there are no errors or genuine contradictions in the biblical text, but we have not fully explained how we arrive at our conclusion. In this question we will examine some of the principles for dealing with alleged contradictions and errors in the Bible. Why is it important for us to be aware of the claims to alleged contradictions in the Bible or the fact that they can be resolved by giving careful attention to the text? Because far too many people have taken for granted the claims of critics that the biblical accounts have errors or conflict and are thus unreliable, and that therefore the Bible itself must be called into question and cannot be believed. To prove that the Bible does not err or conflict is to give evidence of the historical care and accuracy of those who wrote it. And if the biblical writers were careful writers, then what they say can be trusted.

In the following material we will employ several principles for dealing with alleged discrepancies. Here we briefly describe five common "rules" or observations which the reader should keep in mind. There are others, but these primary ones are given to illustrate that one cannot read Scripture at a surface level only and then logically conclude that contradiction or error exists. Regrettably, religious and secular critics of Christianity, such as atheists, Muslims, Mormons, and humanists, do this all too frequently; e.g., simple differences are claimed as genuine contradictions. But in doing so, the critics characteristically uncover their own methodological errors or biases rather then any scriptural error or contradiction. Indeed, "to use the divergences to cast doubt on the historicity of events on which [all the Gospels] obviously agree is a strange sort of historical methodology."[57] As Dr. Wilbur Smith points out, "Statements directly and positively contradictory to the main point at issue would undoubtedly justify our rejecting it; but where the main point is admitted by every witness, slighter divisions are not only perfectly consistent with its truth, but are of the utmost importance for establishing it."[58]

The vast majority of alleged contradictions or errors result from three factors: 1) too cursory an examination; 2) the faulty methodologies of the critics; or 3) the biblical authors' selective use of data. Careful analysis invariably reveals that no contradiction or error exists. Thus, concerning something like the resurrection narratives, typically the most abused and subject to attack by critics:

> If, after these one hundred years of the sharpest, bitterest, most unmerciful criticism of these records, a criticism more terrifically severe than any other documents have endured, the Resurrection narrative still stands unshaken,

unmutilated, unharmed, men ought to be persuaded that the things here spoken of are according to the truth. . . .[59]

In fact, given the principles listed below, almost all the alleged contradictions or errors in the Bible are resolved merely by a careful evaluation of the Bible itself. This should tell us something. As Dr. Craig L. Blomberg (Ph.D., University of Aberdeen), Associate Professor of New Testament, Denver Seminary, and author of *The Historical Reliability of the Gospels*, observes for the Gospels, "Virtually all the so-called contradictions in the Gospels can be readily harmonized."[60]

Principle One: The proper definition of a contradiction or error must be observed.

Many people misunderstand the proper definition of terms such as "contradiction" and "error." This is one reason why misunderstanding exists when it comes to alleged errors and contradictions in the Scriptures. The oft-repeated claim of skeptics that there are "hundreds of contradictions" is a result of their failure to abide by proper definitions. When a critic charges that there is an error or contradiction in Scripture the burden of proof rests upon him to prove his claim.

Webster's New World Dictionary of the American Language (College Edition) defines "to contradict" as "1. a) to assert the opposite of (what someone else has said)." This same dictionary defines "error" as "1. the state of believing what is untrue, incorrect, or wrong. 2. a wrong belief; incorrect opinion." The dictionary points out that "error implies deviation from truth, accuracy, correctness, right, etc."

The "principle of noncontradiction" is defined in *Webster's New Twentieth Century Dictionary* (2d ed., 1977) as "the axiom that truth and falsity are never inherent in the same thing simultaneously in the same sense."

If a violation of the above definitions can be proven in Scripture, then a genuine contradiction or error has occurred. This has never been done.

Principle Two: The reader or critic must be fair with the biblical writers and grant them the courtesy he grants to other writers.

As we saw, one rule for examining ancient manuscripts is to assume that the writers were accurate unless sufficient reason exists to disqualify them. This involves no more than the common courtesy of giving the writer the benefit of the doubt until proven otherwise. In 2000 years, the New Testament writers have not been proven to be dishonest or the victims of deception. As the noted biblical scholar F. F. Bruce observes, "There is, I imagine, no body of literature in the world that has been exposed to the stringent analytical study that the four Gospels have sustained for the past 200 years. This is not something to be regretted; it is something to be accepted with satisfaction. Scholars today who trust the Gospels as credible historical documents do so in the full light of this analytical study, not by closing their minds to it."[61]

What more could critics want?

Given such a lengthy span of time in which to discredit the New Testament, the fact that it has not been discredited would certainly indicate its essential integrity. Thus, rather than presuppose error or even fraud, fair-minded scholarship assumes that the writer is being honest until proven otherwise. Dr. Arndt argues as follows:

> Fairness demands that, when we meet two seemingly contradictory statements in an author, we do not exaggerate the differences, but make an honest endeavor to harmonize them. The a priori assumption must always be that the author has not contradicted himself. This rule is observed in dealing with secular authors. At what pains, for instance, have not editors been to bring about agreement between seemingly conflicting statements in the writings of Plato! The principle by which they were guided is that no contradiction must be assumed unless all attempts at harmonizing fail. That is in accordance with the dictates of fairness. Let but the same amount of goodwill be manifested in the treatment of the difficult passages in the Bible, and the charge that it contains irreconcilable discrepancies will no longer be heard.[62]

Principle Three: Informed study must be given to all relevant areas: original languages, history, culture, literary form, etc.

For example, the works of John W. Haley, William Arndt, and Gleason Archer collectively examine over a thousand alleged Bible discrepancies, almost all of which are adequately resolved by careful attention to relevant detail: original languages, immediate and larger contexts, geography, culture, sound principles of literary interpretation, archeological data, specialized use of terms, etc.

Thus, surface discrepancies should never be accepted as genuine errors without sufficient regard to the details of the text itself. It is crucial that an individual not be swayed by first impressions but that he be willing to make a thorough study of the alleged problem, because at times a good deal of study is necessary in order to resolve an apparent contradiction.

Unless one understands what an author has actually stated, he will be unable to interpret him properly. Such misunderstandings lead to false interpretations, which may subsequently lead to charges of contradiction or error.

Everyone knows that the Bible contains a wide variety of literary styles: historical narrative, prophecy, law, gospel, poetry, parable, apocalyptic, and many figurative uses of language: metaphor, hyperbole, simile, allegory, and others. But principles of interpretation that apply to one literary form do not always apply to another. For example, Gordon Fee, Professor of New Testament at Gordon Conwell Theological Seminary, and Douglas Stuart, Professor of Old Testament at Gordon Conwell, observe in *How to Read the Bible for All It's Worth* that different biblical genres require different exegetical questions and skills. They show how easy it is to misunderstand the biblical text:

> At its highest level, of course, exegesis requires knowledge of many things . . . the biblical languages; the Jewish, Semitic, and Hellenistic backgrounds; how to determine the original text when the manuscripts have variant readings; the use of all kinds of primary sources and tools. . . . The key to good exegesis, and therefore to a more intelligent reading of the Bible, is *to learn to read the text carefully and to ask the right questions of the text.* One of the best things one could do in this regard would be to read Mortimer J. Adler's *How to Read a Book* (1940, rev. ed., with Charles Van Doren, New York: Simon and Schuster, 1972). Our experience over many years in college and seminary teaching is that many people simply do not know how to read well. To read or study the Bible intelligently demands careful reading, and that includes learning to ask the right questions of the text.[63]

For example, even the simple name of an apostle can present apparent contradictions. The apostle Peter is given the following names in Scripture: Peter, Cephas, Simeon, Simon, Simon Peter, Simon Bar-jona, and Simon son of Jonas. To confuse them with someone else may lead to a seeming contradiction.

Fee and Stuart continue to illustrate the importance of careful study by offering the following examples:

> It simply makes a difference in understanding to know the personal background of Amos, Hosea, or Isaiah, or

that Haggai prophesied *after* the exile, or to know the messianic expectations of Israel when John the Baptist and Jesus appeared on the scene, or to understand the differences between the cities of Corinth and Philippi and how these affect the churches in each. One's reading of Jesus' parables is greatly enhanced by knowing something about the customs of Jesus' day. Surely it makes a difference in understanding to know that the "penny" (KJV), or denarius, offered to the workers in Matthew 20:1-16 was the equivalent of a full day's wage. Even matters of topography are important. One who was raised in the American West—or East for that matter—must be careful not to think of "the mountains that surround Jerusalem" (Ps. 125:2) in terms of his or her own experience of mountains![64]

Principle Four: Mere differences do not equal contradictions.

All writers have the right to select those facts that fit their purposes and disregard others. Critics who will not accept this principle are applying a standard to the biblical writers that they would apply to no one else, including themselves. For example, Numbers 25:9 declares that a total of 24,000 people died in a plague of divine judgment. When citing this incident the apostle Paul declares that 23,000 of them died "in one day" (1 Corinthians 10:8). Clearly the other thousand took longer to die than one day. Paul's emphasis here is on the suddenness of the judgment. Yet many critics have cited these verses as a biblical contradiction, either not reading the texts carefully or neglecting the fact that mere differences do not necessarily equal contradictions or errors.

John W. Haley discusses this cause of apparent discrepancies, which is particularly relevant for the resurrection narratives:

> Many other apparent discrepancies, of a historical character, are occasioned by the adoption, by the several authors, of different principles and methods of arrangement. One writer follows the strict chronological order; another disposes his materials according to the principle of association of ideas. One writes history minutely and consecutively; another omits, condenses, or expands to suit his purpose. . . . The methods of the several authors being thus different, it cannot but be that their narratives, when compared, will present appearances of dislocation, deficiency, redundancy, anachronism, or even antagonism—one or all of these. . . . Nor is an author's omission

34

to mention an event equivalent to a denial of that event. It should also be remembered that a writer may imply customary phraseology, involving a historical inaccuracy, yet not be chargeable with falsehood, inasmuch as he does not intend to teach anything in reference to the matter. For example, a historian might incidentally speak of the "battle of Bunker Hill," while he knows perfectly well the battle was fought on Breed's Hill.[65]

Principle Five: The limitations on human knowledge should be granted.

Over the centuries, biblical critics have frequently offered "proof" of error in Scripture by appealing to various names, numbers, dates, events, etc. which were found in the Bible alone. In other words, because no extrabiblical confirmation could be found an error was assumed. Examples include the civilization of the Hittites (Genesis 10:15), King Sargon (Isaiah 20:1), and Darius the Mede (Daniel 5:31).

But to be fair, one must assume that an author who has already established his credibility remains credible even even when something he has said cannot directly be proven from other sources. Time and again the biblical authors have proven their accuracy. It is thus far more logical to assume that further information will sustain their credibility than destroy it. Indeed, this is exactly what we find. Every alleged error or contradiction in Scripture has been proven a truthful statement once sufficient archeological, linguistic, or other information has been discovered. This gives one great confidence that problems currently unresolvable for lack of data will eventually have a similar outcome.

6. What can an ancient Egyptian noble tell us about the Bible today?

The first five books of the Bible, known collectively as the Pentateuch, set the tone for the rest of the Bible. These books claim to be a divine revelation written by Moses, who was adopted by the Pharaoh's daughter, treated as her son, and thus probably educated in the Pharaoh's own court (Acts 7:21,22). Later he became the leader of the famed Jewish exodus. His five books record everything from the creation, fall, and flood to the lives of the patriarchs, the exodus, and the giving of the Mosaic law—which greatly influenced the course of Western civilization, including modern law and ethics.

If these books are fraudulent, then so is the rest of the Old Testament which is so integrally related to them. (For example, without the legitimacy of the divine law given by Moses, intended to keep Israel from corruption by her pagan neighbors, the entire Old Testament ministry of the prophets becomes useless.) The truth is that the credibility of the entire Old Testament stands or falls upon the legitimacy of its first five books. If these books are questionable, so is the entire Old Testament. And if the Old Testament can be doubted, no one can logically believe in the authority of the New Testament either. (For example, Jesus clearly claimed He was the prophesied Messiah of the Old Testament and that the God of the Old Testament was His Father. He believed the that the Old Testament was the inerrant Word of God. If He was wrong on such crucial matters, what could He be right on?)

Thus the legitimacy of Christianity itself is logically dependent upon the credibility of the Pentateuch and its claim to divine origin. Christians maintain that the historical evidence supporting the claims of the Pentateuch is solidly on their side. Biblical critics argue otherwise—that not only did Moses not write the Pentateuch, but even that he couldn't have written it. They put forth their theories under the name "The documentary hypothesis." Who is right and who is wrong?

The critical view holds that the Pentateuch was not inspired by God through Moses but was written by numerous unknown Palestinian editors from the ninth through the fifth centuries B.C. or later. In their compilation they used four principal source documents (J, E, D, P). The conservative view holds that the Pentateuch was written by Moses in the fifteenth century B.C.

The historical facts document the conservative view of the Pentateuch as being written by Moses in the fifteenth century B.C.

First, the Bible itself indisputably teaches Mosaic authorship. By accepted cannons of historic investigation, the claims of an ancient document must be regarded as legitimate unless shown otherwise. Since the Bible has repeatedly been proven reliable historically (e.g., in archeological discoveries), its consistent testimony to Mosaic authorship should be accepted. The Pentateuch claims Mosaic authorship (Exodus 24:4; Numbers 31:1,2; Deuteronomy 31:9), as do the Prophets (Malachi 4:4), Jesus (John 5:46,47; 7:19), and the apostles (John 1:17; Acts 3:22; 13:39; Romans 10:5; and more). Jesus Himself told His Jewish enemies, "Do not think I will accuse you before the Father. Your accuser is Moses, on whom your hopes are set. If you believed Moses, you would believe me, for he wrote about me. But since you do not believe what he wrote, how are you going to believe what I say?" (John 5:45-47 NIV).

If Moses did not write the Pentateuch, then the Bible is wrong at all these points and more. Jesus was also wrong. Further, both promote blatant deception for declaring that Moses did write it. One wonders why critics would spend millions of man hours defending their rationalistic Pentateuchal theories concerning a document that promotes deception!

Second, the internal data of the Pentateuch (climate, flora and fauna, geography, linguistic data, etc.) show considerable familiarity with fifteenth-century Egyptian life. A thorough and very particular acquaintance with fifteenth-century B.C. Egyptian life and geography would be highly unlikely for ninth- through fifth-century B.C. Israelite editors. But such knowledge would clearly suggest that the author was a resident of Egypt and a contemporary eyewitness of the events recorded.[66] According to the New Testament, "Moses was educated in all the learning of the Egyptians" (Acts 7:22 NASB), so we would expect such knowledge.

Third, Jerusalem is not mentioned by name in the Pentateuch. It is inconceivable that the vital capital city of Jerusalem would not be mentioned even once in extensive Jewish writings of the ninth through the fifth century B.C., not only in light of the alleged diversity of authors, but the very nature of the source documents themselves, especially "P" (the priestly document), which was concerned with the temple worship and sacrifices. On the other hand, if the Pentateuch were written before Jerusalem was the capitol of Israel (1000 B.C.), such absence is expected.

Fourth, Moses was fully qualified in every respect to write the Pentateuch, and Jesus Himself confirmed that He did in fact write it (John 5:47).[67]

Fifth, the assumption of the critic that miracles never occur (the exodus, predictive prophecy, etc.) is not tenable, particularly in light of an objective evaluation of the overall documentation for biblical prophecy (Daniel chapters 2, 7, 11; Isaiah 53: Psalm 22; Micah 5:2). In fact, Pentateuchal predictions of the future Assyrian deportation and judgment of Israel (Leviticus 26; Deuternomy 28) indicates a divine source behind Moses' writings, since much later redactors would be unlikely to write of such a fate for Israel.

Sixth, the cumulative weight of recent archaeological discovery proves the antiquity of the Pentateuch. Hence, in the words of famed archaeologist W. F. Albright, it is "sheer hypercriticism to deny the substantially Mosaic character of the Pentateuchal tradition."[68] Indeed, biblical scholars with impeccable academic credentials, now reject the documentary hypothesis on archeological grounds alone. (In his *Survey of Old*

Testament Introduction and other works, Dr. Gleason Archer has many examples of archeological confirmation of the biblical text in general and Mosaic authorship in particular.)

Seventh, the presence of social customs of the second millennium B.C. are difficult to explain if the Pentateuch was written in the first millennium B.C.[69]

Eighth, the use of the divine names in the Pentateuch, Jehovah and Elohim, depend upon context and have never been successfully construed as proof of divergent sources.[70]

Ninth, the wholly unique monotheistic character of Israelite religion is unexplainable in light of her pagan surroundings, her regular lapses into idolatry, and the data of comparative religion. The alleged gradual social evolution of Israelite religion from polytheism to monotheism is thereby rendered untenable, and with it a supporting pillar of the documentary hypothesis.[71]

Tenth, the amazing unity[72] of the Pentateuch is highly suggestive of a single author. In light of the above data in points 1 through 9, a late editorial harmonizer(s) is not credible.[73]

Eleventh, Jesus Christ, who is God, authenticated the Mosaic authorship. Nowhere did Jesus ever express even the slightest doubt about Mosaic authorship of the Pentateuch or about the divine authority of the entire Old Testament. In one place He spoke of "the Law of Moses" (Luke 24:44 NASB) and in another He asked, "Did not Moses give you the law?" (John 7:19 NASB).

Apparently, critics somehow assume that they are wiser and know more than Jesus.

In conclusion, the documentary hypothesis rejects the divine and Mosaic authorship of the Pentateuch. Yet the theory with real problems is not this one, but the documentary hypothesis itself. Innumerable internal contradictions and reversals characterize both the development and the current formulation(s) of the documentary theory.[74] These include circular reasoning, rationalistic premises, blatant ignoring of contrary data, a priori assumption of biblical error, special pleading, etc. Despite its prominence and popularity, the documentary hypothesis is now, like always, a thoroughly discredited theory.[75] This means that the only rational and credible view is the Christian view which supports the reliability of the Pentateuch.

7. What is the amazing truth about the book of Daniel?

Perhaps no book in the Bible has aroused as much controversy or skepticism as the book of Daniel. It's not difficult to understand why. The prophecies in chapters 2, 7, and 11 are so detailed they would have to be written after the fact if we discount the possibility of predictive prophecy. Yet everyone agrees that the information is there. If Daniel was written when it claims to have been written, then specific, detailed, predictive prophecy is clearly proven and established. That is the amazing truth about the book of Daniel.

According to critics, the book of Daniel is a second century (165 B.C.) text used by a pseudonymous author as a literary device interpreting history retrospectively to encourage Maccabean Jews during the persecution of the Syrian ruler Antiochus Epiphanes IV.

Christians maintain that Daniel is a genuinely prophetic text written by Daniel, a contemporary of Ezekiel, and a captive of the Babylonian King Nebuchadnezzar near the end of his life, about 530 B.C. As such it contains predictive prophecy that is unmistakable in describing the future kingdoms of Medo-Persia, Greece, and Rome.

The following facts document the conservative view.

First, Jesus Christ, being God, is an infallible authority. In referring to "Daniel the Prophet" (Matthew 24:15 NASB; and further documenting this by citing Daniel's still future "abomination of desolation"), Jesus declared both the authenticity of the book and the prophetic office of Daniel, thereby undercutting the principal bias and pillar of the critics' antisupernaturalism.

Second, for Daniel to be mentioned by God three times in the book of Ezekiel (14:14, 20; 28:3), he must at least have been Ezekiel's contemporary or older. Even critics accept Ezekiel as being written in the sixth century B.C. If Daniel was a contemporary of Ezekiel, he could hardly have been born three centuries later. For the liberal to respond by asserting that the Daniel mentioned in Ezekiel was a Baal worshiper, as if to discredit the conservative view, is utterly untenable in light of the intent of the passage and the godly men cited with him.

Third, the author of Daniel consistently places himself in sixth-century B.C. Babylon (e.g., 1:1; 2:1; 5:31; 7:1; 8:1; 9:1; 10:1; 11:1) and declares that divine revelations were given to him (7:2,15; 8:1ff.; 9:2ff.). Further, the linguistic, geographic, cultural, and theological data are consistent with a Babylonian composition (including the existence of earlier Jewish theology). If the author of Daniel claims he is writing in the sixth century and receiving divine revelation, yet is actually writing in the second century and inventing it, he is a liar and should be dismissed. Such a forgery could never have been accorded the status of canonicity by the Jews. Nor would a Jew writing under persecution in 165 B.C. in Judea be likely to fabricate the specific earmarks of the sixth-century B.C. Babylonian period, whether linguistically, geographically, or culturally, or reflect preMaccabean Jewish theology (e.g., angels, resurrection, Messiah, last judgment).

Fourth, the internal unity of the book of Daniel as to style means it could not have been a composite work of different authors and/or editors. Daniel 12:4 implies full authorship by one person.

Fifth, if written in 165 B.C., Daniel could hardly have been previously placed in the Jewish canon that closed in 400 B.C. Given its obvious errors, according to critical dating (e.g., Daniel 11:40-45 is not the manner in which Antiochus Epiphanes met his death), it would not have been canonized even by Maccabean Jews. Further, to have been translated in the Greek translation of the Old Testament, the Septuagint, in 250 B.C., it is impossible for Daniel to have been written in 165 B.C.

Sixth, recently discovered archeological data further supports a Babylonian composition, in confirmation of what the text declares (Daniel 2:12, 13, 46; 6:8, 9; 8:2). A Maccabean Jew writing in 165 B.C. would not be familiar with the specific legal regulations and geographical details of the earlier Babylonian and Medo-Persian pagan empires.

Seventh, Josephus writes that Alexander the Great was shown a copy of the book of Daniel. This occurred some 200 years prior to 165 B.C., when critics allege the book was written. Everyone knows that Alexander the Great lived in the fourth century B.C. He could hardly be shown a book that would not be written for some 200 years.

Eighth, the Qumran scrolls of Psalms and Chronicles must now be dated at least as early as the Persian period (538–333 B.C.); on the exact same criteria Daniel must also be dated no later. Further, a Daniel fragment at Qumran also indicates canonicity; the Maccabean Jews would not have accepted Daniel without a previous history of canonicity.

Ninth, even if the critics' impossible date of 165 B.C. is accepted, we still find predictive prophecy in the book of Daniel in the fourth kingdom of chapters 2 and 7. The facts require that Rome be considered Daniel's fourth kingdom, yet Rome did not come into power until 63 B.C., a century after 165 B.C. The comments of Jerome (347–420 A.D.), who lived in the decline of the Roman Empire, are illuminating at this point. In his commentary on Daniel 2:40 he states:

Now the fourth empire, which clearly refers to the Romans, is the iron empire which breaks in pieces and overcomes all others. But its feet and toes are partly of iron and partly of earthenware, a fact most clearly demonstrated at the present time. For just as there was at the first nothing stronger or hardier than the Roman realm, so also in these last days there is nothing more feeble . . . since we require the assistance of barbarian tribes both in our civil wars and against foreign nations.[76]

In addition, Daniel 9:24-27 contains specific messianic prophecy.[77] Thus, even granting the 165 B.C. date, if the book still contains genuine prophecy, the very basis for the critics' assumption of a late date, the impossibility of predictive prophecy, is undermined.

Tenth, if we argue Daniel was written in 165 B.C., the influence of the Greek language and culture would have been much more pronounced.

Eleventh, the alleged positive evidences for a 165 B.C. date (e.g., placement in the Writings; lack of mention by Jesus ben Sirach; use of the third person; alleged inaccuracies concerning the sixth century B.C.; such literary features as the use of Aramaic; three Greek words for musical instruments in 3:10, and so-called "later" theological content) are all refuted by an unbiased consideration of the data. (The Greek language for example, was known in the time of Daniel.) In fact, most of the errors that the critics find today in Daniel result from their own faulty assumption that Daniel was written in 165 B.C.!

In conclusion, the noted linguistic scholar Dr. R. D. Wilson observes in his still definitive study of Daniel that the critics "have failed to present a single fact of direct evidence in support of [their] positions."[78] This means that the book of Daniel supplies proof of predictive prophecy and is one more evidence of biblical inspiration and reliability.

8. What can skeptics learn about the Bible from science and mathematics?*

Over the years at The John Ankerberg Show we have invited numerous skeptics and critics of the Bible to appear on TV and thus have had to read widely in the skeptical literature. Neither from the guests on our TV show nor from our reading of the literature have we ever found a legitimate argument

---

* A more thorough treatment is found in our *Ready with an Answer* (Harvest House, 1997).

against the Bible that would stand the weight of critical scrutiny.

Skeptics generally don't believe the Bible simply because they don't want to believe it. How do we know this? Because historically, thousands of former skeptics have become Christians on the basis of the evidence for the truth of Christianity. If that evidence didn't exist and weren't persuasive, such individuals would never have become Christians. No amount of evidence will convince someone against his will. But for the open-minded person, the evidence is more than sufficient to establish the truth of Christianity.

Two areas in particular that may interest open-minded agnostics or skeptics are the scientific prevision found in the Bible and the mathematical probability factors in favor of its divine inspiration as seen through messianic prophecy.

Space allows only the briefest comments at this point. However, both of these subjects have been dealt with in more detail in our *Ready with an Answer* and in greater detail by other authors.

Concerning the scientific prevision of the Bible, this is unique in the history of literature. In *The Creator Beyond Time and Space,* medical doctor Mark Eastman and Chuck Missler, a computer specialist, provide many examples showing how the Bible, scientifically speaking, was thousands of years ahead of its time. They point out that "there are dozens of passages in the Bible which demonstrate tremendous scientific foreknowledge."[79] In fact, "when the biblical text is carefully examined the reader will quickly discover an uncanny scientific accuracy unparalleled by any document of antiquity. . . . The Bible does not use scientific jargon nor is it a scientific text per se. However, as we will see, the Bible does describe scientific phenomena in common terminology with unmistakable clarity. . . . In virtually all ancient religious documents it is common to find scientifically inaccurate myths about the nature of the universe and the life forms on planet Earth. Any cursory review of ancient mythology will readily confirm this statement. However, the Bible is unique because of the conspicuous absence of such myths. In fact, throughout the Bible we find scientifically accurate concepts about the physical universe that were not 'discovered' by modern scientists until very recent times."[80] They provide examples from physics, astronomy, oceanography, the earth's hydrologic cycle, meteorology, medicine, geology, and biology. Further, in *The Biblical Basis for Modern Science* (Baker, 1984), scientist Dr. Henry M. Morris offers a 500-page text supplying a large number of additional examples of scientific foreknowledge or allusions in the Bible.

For skeptics to successfully argue that the Bible is not the inspired Word of God, they must explain how the Bible contains statements like this which were often disharmonious with the accepted knowledge of the time in which they were written and yet are completely accurate in light of today's known scientific facts. In essence, to argue that the evidences for biblical inspiration are the result of a huge number of lucky guesses requires an enormous amount of faith because we know that it is impossible for people to write science and history in advance apart from divine inspiration.[81]

When we examine biblical prophecy and mathematical probability, we find further evidence that the Bible is in fact the Word of God. In the Bible, God Himself teaches that His perfect knowledge of the future is proof that He alone is the Lord. No other god or religious scripture has consistently (or even sparingly) told of things to come and also had them come true just as forecast (see Isaiah 41:20-29). Indeed, one reason God says that He has clearly predicted the future is "so that all the peoples of the earth may know that the Lord is God and that there is no other" (1 Kings 8:60 NIV; cf.vv. 1-59).

God Himself says that He accurately predicts the future and that He has done so in order that people may know that He alone is the one true God. His prophets are "recognized as one truly sent by the Lord only if [their] prediction comes true" (Jeremiah 28:9 NIV). God promises, "Whatever I say will be fulfilled, declares the Sovereign Lord" (Ezekiel 12:28 NIV).

In light of the above, consider the following facts: 62 of the 66 books of the Bible contain prophetic material, and if we add the total number of predictive verses in the Bible, we find that their number is amazing: Of 31,124 verses, 8352 are prophetic! This is 27 percent of the entire Bible![82] Ponder this for a moment. For God to have promised that His predictions are accurate and then offered 8352 predictive verses in the Bible, including 1817 total predictions with 737 separate matters predicted, consider how incredibly easy it would be to prove that the Bible is not the Word of God by finding just one false prediction. But in fact no false prediction has ever been proven.

Professor Emeritus of Science at Westmont College, Peter Stoner, has calculated the probability of one man fulfilling the major prophecies made concerning the Messiah. The estimates were worked out by 12 different classes of 600 college students.

The students carefully weighed all the factors, discussed each prophecy at length, and examined the various circumstances which might indicate that men had conspired together to fulfill a particular prophecy. They made their estimates conservative enough so that there was finally unanimous agreement even among the most skeptical students.

But then Professor Stoner took their estimates and made them even more conservative. He also encouraged other skeptics or scientists to make their own estimates to see if his conclusions were more than fair. Finally, he submitted his figures for review to a committee of the American Scientific Affiliation. Upon examination, they verified that his calculations were dependable and accurate in regard to the scientific material presented.[83]

Stoner's calculations concerned only eight different prophecies, but the conservatively estimated chance of one man fulfilling all eight prophecies was 1 in 10^{17}. In another calculation, Stoner used 48 prophecies and arrived at the extremely conservative estimate that the probability of 48 prophecies being fulfilled in one person is 10^{157}.[84]

Anyone who ponders the size of a number like 10^{157} will prove to himself what experts in probability theory have always maintained: An event whose odds are only 1 chance in 10^{157} will never occur naturalistically.[85] Mathematical facts, then, force us to invoke divine power to explain biblical prophecy.

All of this means that it is impossible for these 48 prophecies of Stoner's to be fulfilled by chance alone. But then what of several hundred other prophecies? All this is proof that there must be a God who supernaturally gave this information and that this God is the God of the Bible. He alone is the one true God who created us. But if so, then how important it is for us to come to know Him personally!

Our eternal destiny depends on whether or not we believe in Jesus Christ as our personal Savior (Matthew 20:28; 25:46; 26:28; John 3:16-18, 36; 5:24). Jesus Himself emphasized, "I told you that you would die in your sins; if you do not believe that I am the one I claim to be, you will indeed die in your sins" (John 8:24 NIV).

The Bible teaches that "all have sinned and fall short of the glory of God" and that "the wages of sin is death, but the free gift of God is eternal life in Christ Jesus our Lord" (Romans 3:23; 6:23 NASB). Because we have sinned and broken God's laws, we need His forgiveness before we can enter into a personal relationship with Him and inherit eternal life. This gift is free. Anyone who wishes can receive Christ as his or her personal Savior by praying the following prayer (the exact words are not important, but you may wish to use this prayer as a guide):

> Dear God, I confess I am a sinner who has broken Your laws. I now turn from my sins. I ask Jesus Christ to enter my life. I now choose to make Him my Lord and my Savior. I realize that this is a serious decision and commitment, and I do not enter into it lightly. I believe that on the cross Jesus Christ died for my sins, then rose from the dead three days later. I receive Him as my eternal King. Help me to live my life so it is pleasing to You. Amen.

Again, accepting Christ is a serious commitment. If you have prayed this prayer we encourage you to write us at The John Ankerberg Show for help in growing as a Christian. We suggest the following. Begin to read a modern, easy-to-read translation of the Bible (such as the New International Version or the New American Standard Bible). Start with the New Testament, Psalms and Proverbs and then proceed to the rest of the Scriptures. Also, find a church where people honor the Bible and God's Word and Christ as Lord and Savior. Tell someone of your decision to follow Christ and begin to grow in your new relationship with God by talking to Him daily in prayer. Then continue to read the Bible daily, as well as good Christian literature. This will help you to "grow in the grace and knowledge of our Lord and Savior Jesus Christ" (2 Peter 3:18 NIV). Seek out all you can about "the eternal life to which you were called" (1 Timothy 6:12) and which you have just begun. Take your Lord seriously and enjoy Him immensely, since your relationship will last forever, and "no eye has seen, no ear has heard, no mind has conceived what God has prepared for those who love him" (1 Corinthians 2:9 NIV).

Summary: The Uniqueness of the Bible

1. The Bible is the only book in the world that offers objective evidence to be the Word of God. Only the Bible gives real proof of its divine inspiration.

2. The Bible is the only religious Scripture in the world that is inerrant.

3. The Bible is the only ancient book with documented scientific and medical prevision. No other ancient book is ever carefully analyzed along scientific lines, but many modern books have been written on the theme of the Bible and modern science.

4. The Bible is the only religious writing that offers eternal salvation as a free gift entirely by God's grace and mercy.

5. The Bible is the only major ancient religious writing whose complete textual preservation is established as virtually autographic.

6. The Bible contains the greatest moral standards of any book.

7. Only the Bible begins with the creation of the universe by divine fiat and contains a continuous, if often brief and interspersed, historical record of mankind from the first man, Adam, to the end of history.

8. Only the Bible contains detailed prophecies about the coming Savior of the world, prophecies which have proven true in history.

9. Only the Bible has a totally realistic view of human nature, the power to convict people of their sin, and the ability to change human nature.

10. Only the Bible has unique theological content, including its theology proper (the trinity; God's attributes); soteriology (depravity, imputation, grace, propitiation atonement, reconciliation, regeneration, union with Christ, justification, adoption, sanctification, eternal security, election, etc.); Christology (the incarnation, hypostatic union); pneumatology (the Person and work of the Holy Spirit); eschatology (detailed predictions of the end of history); ecclesiology (the nature of the church as Christ's bride and in a spiritually organic union with Him); etc.

11. Only the Bible offers a realistic and permanent solution to the problem of human sin and evil.

12. Only the Bible has its accuracy confirmed in history by archeology, science, etc.

13. The internal and historical characteristics of the Bible are unique in its unity and internal consistency despite production over a 1500-year period by 40-plus authors in three languages on three continents discussing scores of controversial subjects, yet having agreement on all issues.

14. The Bible is the most translated, purchased, memorized, and persecuted book in history. For example, it has been translated into some 1700 languages.

15. Only the Bible is fully one-quarter prophetic, containing a total of some 400 complete pages of predictions.

16. Only the Bible has withstood 2000 years of intense scrutiny by critics and not only survived the attacks but prospered and had its credibility strengthened by such criticism. (Voltaire predicted that the Bible would be extinct within 100 years, but within 50 years Voltaire was extinct and his house was a warehouse for the Bibles of the Geneva Bible Society.)

17. Only the Bible has molded the history of Western civilization more than any other book. The Bible has had more influence in the world than any other book.

18. Only the Bible has a Person-specific (Christ-centered) nature for each of its 66 books, detailing the Person's life in prophecy, type, antitype, etc., 400 to 1500 years before that Person was ever born.

19. Only the Bible proclaims a resurrection of its central figure that can be proven in history.

20. Only the Bible provides historic proof that the one true God loves mankind.

Notes

1. Citations taken from Frank S. Meade, *The Encyclopedia of Religious Quotations*; Rhoda Tripp, *The International Thesaurus of Quotations*; Ralph L. Woods, *The World Treasury of Religious Quotations*; Jonathan Green, *Morrow's International Dictionary of Contemporary Quotations*.
2. Paul D. Feinberg, "The Meaning of Inerrancy," in Norman L. Geisler, *Inerrancy* (Grand Rapids: The Zondervan Corporation, 1979, 1980), p. 294.
3. Ibid., p. 296.
4. John Ankerberg and John Weldon, *Ready with an Answer* (Eugene, OR: Harvest House, 1997), ch. 15.
5. Norman L. Geisler and William E. Nix, *A General Introduction to the Bible* (Chicago: Moody Press, 1971), pp. 66-67.
6. Ibid., p. 87.
7. Ibid., p. 88.
8. Ibid., pp. 91, 97.
9. Gleason Archer, *A Survey of Old Testament Introduction*, revised edition (Chicago: Moody Press, 1974), chs. 23-24, 28-29.
10. Cf. John Walvoord, *Daniel: The Key to the Prophetic Revelation* (Chicago: Moody Press, 1960), ch. 11.
11. See our *Knowing the Truth About the Resurrection*; William Lane Craig, *The Son Rises* (Chicago: Moody Press, 1981), especially pp. 88, 124, 133-41.
12. Pinchas Lapide, *The Resurrection of Jesus* (Minneapolis: Augsburg, 1983), pp. 92, 144, 149-50, although he also equivocates on the bodily resurrection (pp. 126-31).
13. John Warwick Montgomery, *The Shape of the Past* (Minneapolis: Bethany, 1975), pp. 138-39; R. C. Sproul, "The Case of Inerrancy: A Methodological Analysis," in Montgomery, ed., *God's Inerrant Word* (Minneapolis: Bethany, 1974), p. 248; cf. 248-60.
14. Chauncey Sanders, *An Introduction to Research in English Literary History* (New York: MacMillan, 1952), p. 160. His comments were specifically in reference to the authenticity or authorship of a given text.
15. Ibid., pp. 143ff.
16. Josh McDowell, *Evidence That Demands a Verdict*, rev. 1979, pp. 39-52; and Geisler and Nix, *General Introduction*, pp. 238, 357-367.
17. McDowell, *Evidence*, p. 42; Newman, "Easter Week Narratives," in Montgomery, ed., *Evidence for Faith*, 281-84.
18. F. F. Bruce, *The Books and the Parchments* (Old Tappan, NJ: Revell, 1963), p. 78.
19. F. F. Bruce, *The New Testament Documents: Are They Reliable?* (Downer's Grove, IL: InterVarsity Press, 1971), p. 15.
20. McDowell, *Evidence*, pp. 43-45; Clark Pinnock, *Biblical Revelation: The Foundation of Christian Theology* (Chicago: Moody Press, 1971), pp. 238-39, 365-66.
21. Robert C. Newman, "Miracles and the Historicity of the Easter Week Narratives," in Montgomery, ed., *Evidence for Faith*, p. 284.
22. See John Warwick Montgomery, *Faith Founded on Fact* (New York: Nelson, 1978); F. F. Bruce, *The New Testament Documents: Are They Reliable?*; John

Warwick Montgomery, *History and Christianity*; Norman Geisler, *Christian Apologetics* (Grand Rapids: Baker, 1976), pp. 322-27.

23. William M. Ramsay, *The Bearing of Recent Discovery on the Trustworthiness of the New Testament* (Grand Rapids: Baker, 1959), p. 81; cf. William F. Ramsay, *Luke the Physician*, pp. 177-79, 222, as given in F. F. Bruce, *The New Testament Documents: Are They Reliable?*, pp. 90-91.

24. A. N. Sherwin-White, *Roman Society and Roman Law in the New Testament* (Oxford: Clarendon Press, 1963), from Geisler, *Christian Apologetics*, p. 326.

25. Gary R. Habermas, *Ancient Evidence for the Life of Jesus: Historical Records of His Death and Resurrection* (New York: Nelson, 1984), p. 66.

26. Philip Schaff and Henry Wace, eds., *A Select Library of Nicene and Post-Nicene Fathers of the Christian Church*, 2d series, vol. 1, Eusebius: Church History, book 3, chapter 39, "The Writings of Papias" (Grand Rapids: Eerdmans, 1976), pp. 172-73.

27. Habermas, *Ancient Evidence*, pp. 66, 177.

28. Ibid., pp. 112-15.

29. Ibid., p. 112.

30. Ibid., pp. 112-13.

31. See our chapter on archeology in *Ready with an Answer*; F. F. Bruce, "Are the New Testament Documents Still Reliable?" in *Christianity Today*, October 28, 1978, pp. 28-33; F. F. Bruce, *The New Testament Documents: Are They Reliable?*, chs. 7-8; Ramsay, *The Bearing of Recent Discoveries*; C. A. Wilson, *Rocks, Relics and Biblical Reliability* (Grand Rapids, Zondervan, 1977), ch. 2; *New Light on New Testament Letters and New Light on the Gospels* (Grand Rapids: Baker, 1975); Edwin Yamauchi, *The Stones and the Scriptures*, Section II (New York: Lippincott, 1972).

32. Wilson, *Rocks, Relics*, p. 120.

33. See any complete concordance listing under "witness," "eyewitness," etc.

34. John Wenham, *Redating Matthew, Mark & Luke* (Downer's Grove, IL: 1992), pp. 115-19, 136, 183, see also pp. xxv, 198, 147, 200, 221, 223, 238-39, 243-45.

35. John A. T. Robinson, *Redating the New Testament* (Philadelphia: Westminster, 1976).

36. In Richard S. Ostling, "Who Was Jesus?" in *Time*, August 15, 1988, p. 41, emphasis added.

37. F. F. Bruce, "Are the New Testament Documents Still Reliable?", p. 33; cf. Craig Blomberg, *The Historical Reliability of the Gospels*, (Downer's Grove, IL: InterVarsity, 1987), pp. 247, 253.

38. Reprinted in John Warwick Montgomery, *The Law Above the Law* (Minneapolis: Bethany, 1975), appendix, pp. 91-140.

39. Reprinted in *The Simon Greenleaf Law Review*, vol. 1 (Orange, CA: The Faculty of the Simon Greenleaf School of Law, 1981–1982), pp. 15-74.

40. Irwin Linton, *A Lawyer Examines the Bible* (San Diego: Creation Life-Publishers, 1977), p. 45.

41. J. N. D. Anderson, *Christianity: The Witness of History* (Downer's Grove, IL: InterVarsity, 1970), pp. 13-14.

42. Citing Henry Morris, *The Bible and Modern Science* (Chicago: Moody Press, 1956, rev.), p. 95, in Josh McDowell, *More Evidence That Demands a Verdict* (Arrowhead Springs, CA: Campus Crusade for Christ, 1975), p. 70.

43. Clifford Wilson, *Archeology, the Bible and Christ*, vol. XVII: Archeological Outlines and a Final Survey (Victory, Australia: Pacific Christian Ministries, 1995), p. 62.

44. Wilson, *Rocks, Relics*, pp.124-25.

45. Robert W. Funk, Roy W. Hoover, and The Jesus Seminar, *The Five Gospels: The Search for the Authentic Words of Jesus* (New York: Macmillan, 1993), p. 34.

46. Montgomery, *Shape of the Past*, p. 176.

47. Gleason Archer, *Encyclopedia of Bible Difficulties* (Grand Rapids: Zondervan, 1982), pp. 11-12.

48. Robert Dick Wilson, *Scientific Investigation of the Old Testament*, pp. 13, 20, 130,162-63; David Otis Fuller, ed., *Which Bible?* (Grand Rapids: Grand Rapids International Publications, rev. 1971, 2d edition), p. 44.

49. John W. Haley, *Alleged Discrepancies of the Bible* (Grand Rapids: Baker, 1982, rpt.), p. vii.

50. William Arndt, *Does the Bible Contradict Itself?* (St. Louis: Concordia, 1955, rpt.), p. XI.

48

51. Harold Lindsell, *The Bible in the Balance* (Grand Rapids: Zondervan, 1979), p. 282.
52. Norman L. Geisler, "Philosophical Presuppositions of Biblical Errancy," in Geisler, ed., *Inerrancy* (Grand Rapids: Zondervan), pp. 306, 319-20. See also Maier, *The End of the Historical-Critical Method*, pp. 11-50.
53. J. Barton Payne, "Higher Criticism and Biblical Inerrancy," in Geisler, *Inerrancy*, p. 333.
54. J. I. Packer cited in Lindsell, *Bible in the Balance*, p. 282.
55. Lindsell, *Bible in the Balance*, p. 301.
56. John Warwick Montgomery, *Faith Founded on Fact* (New York: Thomas Nelson, 1978), p. 47.
57. Newman, "Miracles and the Historicity," in Montgomery, *Evidence for Faith*, 294.
58. Wilbur Smith, *The Supernaturalness of Christ* (Grand Rapids: Baker, 1974, rpt.), p. 205.
59. Ibid., p. 221.
60. Craig L. Blomberg, "Where Do We Start Studying Jesus?" in Michael J. Wilkins and J. P. Moreland, eds., *Jesus Under Fire: Modern Scholarship Reinvents the Historical Jesus* (Grand Rapids, 1995), p. 44.
61. F. F. Bruce, Foreword in Blomberg, *The Historical Reliability*, p. ix.
62. W. Arndt, *Does the Bible Contradict Itself? A Discussion of Alleged Contradictions in the Bible* (St. Louis: Concordia, 5th ed. rev. 1955), p. vi.
63. Gordon Fee and Douglas Stuart, *How to Read the Bible for All It's Worth: A Guide to Understanding the Bible* (Grand Rapids: Zondervan, 1982), pp. 22-23.
64. Ibid., p. 23.
65. Haley, *Alleged Discrepancies*, pp. 9-11.
66. Gleason Archer, *Encyclopedia of Bible Difficulties*, pp. 46-50.
67. Ibid., pp. 51-52; and Gleason Archer, *A Survey of Old Testament Introduction* (Chicago: Moody Press, 1974), p. 118.
68. Archer, *Survey*, p. 176.
69. Ibid., pp. 116-17, 121.
70. Ibid., p. 121.
71. Ibid., chs. 11–21, especially pp. 142-45.
72. Ibid., p. 117.
73. Ibid., pp. 117-18.
74. Ibid., p. 90 and chs. 7–13.
75. Ibid., pp. 105-09, 127-31, 162-63.
76. Gleason Archer, trans., *Jerome's Commentary on Daniel* (Baker, 1977), p. 32.
77. See Robert Anderson, *The Coming Prince* (Kregel); A. J. McClain, *Daniel's Prophecy of the 70 Weeks* (Zondervan); John Walvoord, *Daniel: The Key to Prophetic Revelation*.
78. R. D. Wilson, *Studies in the Book of Daniel*, vol. II, p. 280, rpt., Baker 1979.
79. Mark Eastman and Chuck Missler, *The Creator Beyond Time and Space* (Costa Mesa, CA: The Word for Today, 1996), p. 23.
80. Ibid., p. 87.
81. Ibid., p. 101.
82. See J. Barton Payne, *Encyclopedia of Biblical Prophecy*, pp. 13, 681.
83. Peter W. Stoner, *Science Speaks: Scientific Proof of the Accuracy of Prophecy and the Bible* (Chicago: Moody Press, 1969), p. 4.
84. Ibid., p. 109.
85. Emile Borel, *Probabilities and Life*, chs. 1, 3.